CIVIL WAR
HIGHLIGHTS

THE
CONFEDERACY
ADVANCES
1861–1862

TIM COOKE

A+
Smart Apple Media

This edition published in 2013 by
Smart Apple Media, an imprint of Black Rabbit Books
PO Box 3263, Mankato, MN 56002

www.blackrabbitbooks.com

Brown Bear Books Ltd.
Editorial Director: Lindsey Lowe
Managing Editor: Tim Cooke
Children's Publisher: Anne O'Daly
Picture Manager: Sophie Mortimer
Creative Director: Jeni Child

Library of Congress Cataloging-in-Publication Data
The Confederacy advances : 1861-1862 / edited by Tim Cooke.
    pages cm. -- (Civil War highlights)
 Includes bibliographical references and index.
 Summary: "Contains chronological articles describing the advance
of the Confederate forces during the first 2 years of the US Civil War.
Includes a timeline and study features to help students glean important
information"--Provided by publisher.
 ISBN 978-1-59920-814-5 (library binding)
 1. United States--History--Civil War, 1861-1865--Campaigns--Juvenile
literature. I. Cooke, Tim, 1961-, editor.
 E470.C698 2013
 973.7'3--dc23
                                      2012001163

Printed in the United States of America at Corporate Graphics,
North Mankato, Minnesota

PO1437
2-2012

9 8 7 6 5 4 3 2 1

Picture Credits

Front Cover: Library of Congress

Corbis: Bettmann 15; **Library of Congress:** 4, 5, 7, 10, 11, 14,
16, 18, 20, 21, 23, 24, 25, 26, 27, 30, 32, 33, 34, 36, 37, 40,
42, 43; **National Archives of America:** 6, 8, 13, 19, 31, 38;
Robert Hunt Library: 12, 35.

All Artworks: Windmill Books.

Contents

Introduction

At the start of the conflict, many people in the North believed that the Civil War would soon be over. They thought the North's superior industry and larger population would lead to a quick victory.

The North enjoyed many advantages over the South. It had more people to draft into the army, more railroads to enable it to move troops around, and more factories to make weapons. But the South had more experienced horsemen and hunters to draft into service. And Southerners were eager to fight to defend their lifestyle and homes against what they saw as enemy invaders. In July 1861 Union forces were badly defeated in the first major battle of the war, at Bull Run. The defeat shocked Union supporters. It made it obvious that the war would not be over quickly.

The Union planned to starve the Confederacy of resources by using a naval blockade to prevent any imports or exports

New Orleans fell to the Union in spring 1862, as part of the strategy of gaining control of the Mississippi.

The Battle of Shiloh in April 1861 saw the first large-scale fighting in the West.

from Southern ports. For the South it was crucial to win a rapid victory before the Union's greater resources could give it an advantage.

In the first 18 months of the conflict, the Union managed to get control of the Mississippi in the West, threatening to split the South. But the Confederacy managed to push back a Union advance on the capital in Richmond, Virginia, and was able to invade Northern territory.

In this book

The Confederacy Advances describes the most important engagements of the first two years of the war. A timeline that runs across the bottom of the pages throughout the book traces the course of the whole war on the battlefield, together with other developments in North America and the rest of the world. At the back of the book is a Need to Know feature, which will help you relate subjects to your studies at school.

First Battle of Bull Run (Manassas)

The first major battle of the Civil War was fought on July 21, 1861, near Manassas Junction in northern Virginia. Both sides still believed that the war would be a short conflict.

Wounded soldiers leave the Union lines at the First Battle of Bull Run.

In the North, in particular, the public believed the Union would win a relatively easy victory over the Confederacy. They did not anticipate high casualties. The Battle of Bull Run (known in the South as Manassas) proved such optimism wrong.

1861
January–March

CIVIL WAR

JANUARY 2, SOUTH CAROLINA Fort Johnson in Charleston Harbor is occupied by Confederate troops.

JANUARY 5, ALABAMA Alabama troops seize forts Morgan and Gaines, giving Confederate forces control of Mobile Bay.

JANUARY 9, MISSISSIPPI Leaders vote to leave the Union. Mississippi is the second state to join the Confederacy.

JANUARY 10, FLORIDA Florida leaves the Union.

JANUARY 11, ALABAMA Alabama leaves the Union.

OTHER EVENTS

JANUARY 15, UNITED STATES Engineer Elisha Otis invents the safety elevator.

JANUARY 29, UNITED STATES Kansas joins the Union as the 34th state.

January

Inexperienced armies

The commander of the main Union army was General Irvin McDowell. He had a force of 35,000 men. Many were volunteer militia, however, and McDowell believed that they were not ready to go into battle. The pressure was on McDowell to achieve results, however. The public in the North were eager to fight. In addition, McDowell's volunteers had enlisted for only a year or less, increasing the pressure for a quick resolution. In early July, President Abraham Lincoln ordered McDowell to set out toward the Confederate capital at Richmond, Virginia.

The Battle of Wilson's Creek on August 10, 1861, marked the start of the war in the state of Missouri.

Facing the Union advance were 20,000 equally inxperienced Confederate soldiers. Commanded by Pierre G.T. Beauregard, the army occupied a position just north of Manassas Junction. The settlement stood on Bull Run Creek, only 30 miles (48 km) from Washington, D.C. It was a key Confederate supply depot on the railroad between northern and western Virginia. To the west, Union General Robert Patterson was in the Shenandoah Valley with 18,000 troops. His task was to prevent the 12,000 Confederates of General Joseph E. Johnston moving from the Shenandoah Valley to support Beauregard.

On July 16 McDowell sent a force to capture a Confederate detachment northeast of Manassas, at Fairfax Court House. As he had feared, however, his inexperienced men were not able to carry out even simple maneuvers. The Confederates at Fairfax

JANUARY 19, GEORGIA
Georgia votes to leave the Union.

JANUARY 26, LOUISIANA
Louisiana becomes the sixth state to leave the Union.

FEBRUARY 4, ALABAMA
Leaders from the South meet in the state capital, Montgomery. They choose Jefferson Davis of Mississippi as their president and write a constitution for the Confederate States of America.

FEBRUARY 7, ALABAMA/MISSISSIPPI
The Choctaw Indian Nation forms an alliance with the South. Other Indian tribes follow later.

FEBRUARY, UNITED STATES
The first moving picture system is patented.

MARCH, RUSSIA
Czar Alexander II abolishes serfdom (a form of slavery).

February

March

African American workers build defenses along a Union railroad at Alexandria, Virginia.

STONEWALL JACKSON

Confederate General Thomas "Stonewall" Jackson acquired his famous nickname after his Virginia Brigade held their position during a Union attack on Henry Hill during the First Battle of Bull Run. Observers said the Virginians were standing "like a stone wall."

were easily able to escape to the main lines at Bull Run as the Union forces approached.

With McDowell nearby, Beauregard asked Johnston to reinforce him. Johnston gave Patterson the slip. On July 18 he began using the railroad to move his men. Three days later, the two Confederate armies were united at Manassas.

Contact between the armies

By the time Johnston arrived, the armies had already been skirmishing. On July 18 groups from both sides clashed at Blackburn's Ford, one of six crossing points of Bull Run. In a fight that lasted most of the afternoon, The Confederate troops positioned along the creek resisted a Union advance and held the line on the south side of Bull Run.

Both armies spent the next two days sending out patrols to learn the enemy position as they made their own battle plans for July 21. McDowell planned to turn the enemy's left flank. He would split the two Confederate armies, forcing them to retreat. By chance, Beauregard had also decided to attack his opponent's left flank. His spies in Washington had provided him with accurate information on the positions of the Union army, and Beauregard believed the left flank to be weaker.

Main battle

McDowell attacked first on July 21. He sent 13,000 men across Bull Run at Sudley Ford in a flanking movement. Seeing the danger, the Confederates rushed to oppose them. They waged a bitter fight with Union troops on Matthew's Hill. For many of

1861 April–June

CIVIL WAR

APRIL 12, SOUTH CAROLINA Confederates fire on Fort Sumter in Charleston Harbor in the first shots of the Civil War.

APRIL 15, THE NORTH President Lincoln calls for 75,000 recruits across the North to fight the South.

APRIL 19, WASHINGTON, D.C. President Lincoln declares a naval blockade of Southern states.

APRIL 19, BALTIMORE Mayor George Brown bans Union troops from the city after they are attacked by an angry pro-Confederate mob.

OTHER EVENTS

APRIL, EGYPT A search party sets out from Cairo to find the explorers John Speke and James Grant, who have gone missing while looking for the source of the Nile River.

April

the men on both sides, this was the first time they had been in combat. Many were terrified and uncertain of what to do.

By late morning, the Union soldiers had pushed the enemy back to positions on Henry Hill. The Confederates were almost defeated, if not for the arrival of "Stonewall" Jackson's brigade. By evening, Union forces were retreating toward Washington. They were accompanied by panicking civilians who had come out in the hopes of watching a spectacular Union victory.

In terms of casualties, Bull Run would be dwarfed by later battles. The Union had 2,800 men killed or wounded, the Confederates 1,900. But the battle had ended all illusions that the war would be a quick or bloodless conflict.

BATTLE DETAILS

1. The first contact came on July 18 at Blackburn's Ford. A Union detachment fought Confederate defenders all afternoon before retiring.

2. On July 21 the main Union force advanced at 9:30 A.M. It crossed Bull Run at Sudley Ford to try to outflank the Confederates. By late in the morning, the Confederates had been pushed back to Henry Hill.

3. Fighting continued on Henry Hill. The Confederates were reinforced by Jackson, and counterattacked. By late afternoon the Union troops were fleeing back toward Washington, D.C.

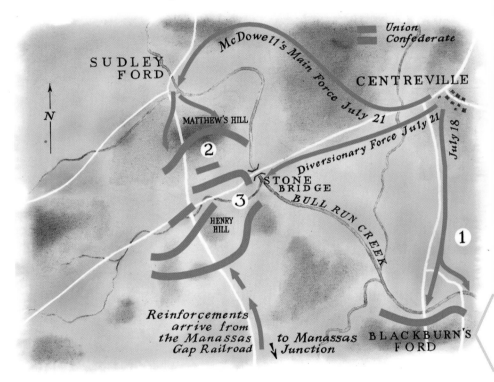

This map shows the movement of the Confederate and Union forces.

APRIL 23, VIRGINIA Major General Robert E. Lee becomes commander of land and naval forces in Virginia.

APRIL 27, WASHINGTON, D.C. Abraham Lincoln suspends "habeus corpus," a law that protects individuals from being arrested.

MAY 9, GREAT BRITAIN Britain announces it will remain neutral in the Civil War.

MAY 20, NORTH CAROLINA North Carolina is the last state to leave the Union.

JUNE 20, VIRGINIA West Virginia is unhappy at Virginia's decision to leave the Union. It breaks from the Confederacy and is admitted into the Union.

APRIL, AUSTRALIA Robert Burke and William Wills, who led the first expedition across Australia, narrowly miss a rendezvous with their colleagues; Burke and Wills will die in the Outback.

JUNE, WASHINGTON, D.C. "Aeronaut" Thaddeus Lowe demonstrates his hot-air balloon for President Abraham Lincoln.

Fight for the Rivers

Union strategy involved the control of the Mississippi River.
In February 1862 this came a step closer as the North won its first
major victories, capturing key forts on two critical rivers.

Union gunboats bombard Fort Henry from the Tennessee River on February 6, 1862.

Forts Henry and Donelson had been built by the Confederates in 1861. They guarded, respectively, the Tennessee and Cumberland Rivers. The forts were part of a Confederate defensive line that stretched across Kentucky from

1861
July—September

CIVIL WAR

JULY 2, WISCONSIN
Union forces push back Confederates near Hainesville in the Battle of Hoke's Run.

JULY 6, CUBA The Confederate raiding ship CSS *Sumter* captures seven vessels in Cuban waters.

JULY 21, VIRGINIA The first major battle of the war is fought at Manassas/First Bull Run. Confederates led by Pierre G.T. Beauregard defeat General Irvin McDowell's larger Union army.

OTHER EVENTS

JULY, UNITED STATES
The Pony Express arrives in San Francisco, beginning a cross-contry mail service.

JULY, UNITED STATES
Congress approves the printing of the first dollar bills, known as "greenbacks."

July

the Mississippi River to the Appalachian foothills. The Tennessee and the Cumberland controlled access to much of Kentucky and Tennessee, so Union commanders planned to seize the forts. On February 2, 1862, Union ironclad gunboats began to bombard Fort Henry from the river. Meanwhile General Ulysses S. Grant arrived with 17,000 men, having steamed up the Ohio and Tennessee rivers. Facing such odds, the fort commander decided not to waste his 3,000 men. He sent most of them to help Fort Donelson, 12 miles (19 km) away, then surrendered. The Confederate commander-in-chief Albert S. Johnston also sent reinforcements to help Fort Donelson. It had become crucial for both sides.

Thousands of Confederate prisoners were captured during the Union seizure of Fort Donelson.

Fall of Fort Donelson

After a delay for bad weather, Grant set out for Fort Donelson on February 12. The Union gunboats opened fire on the 14th, but the fort's cannons caused them great damage. As Grant got into position, the Confederates tried a counterattack to break the Union lines. Some 5,000 Southern troops escaped, but another 15,000 were trapped and surrendered. The Confederates had also lost between 1,500 and 3,500 men killed or wounded; the Union lost 500 killed, 2,100 wounded, and 220 missing. But now the Tennessee and Cumberland rivers were in Union hands, and the Union had won its first victories.

AUGUST 10, MISSOURI
The Battle of Wilson's Creek is the first major battle on the Mississippi River; it sees the first death of a Union general, Nathaniel Lyon.

SEPTEMBER 3, KENTUCKY
Confederate forces invade Kentucky, ending its neutrality.

SEPTEMBER 12–15, WEST VIRGINIA
General Robert E. Lee's Confederate forces are beaten at the Battle of Cheat Mountain Summit.

SEPTEMBER 19, KENTUCKY
The Battle of Barbourville sees Confederates raid an empty Union guerrilla training base.

AUGUST, UNITED STATES
The U.S. Government introduces the first income tax to raise funds for the war.

August   **September**

Clash of the Ironclads

On March 8—9, 1862, armored ships known as ironclads clashed at Hampton Roads, off Chesapeake Bay in Virginia. Although it was a minor battle, it changed the face of naval warfare forever.

The CSS *Virginia* rams and sinks the 24-gun wooden frigate USS *Cumberland*.

The ironclads had been developed by the Confederacy. They were one of the few examples in which Southern technology was more advanced than that of the North. The South was seeking ways to break the Union naval blockade.

1861
October–December

CIVIL WAR

OCTOBER 21, KENTUCKY 7,000 Union troops defeat Confederates at the Battle of Camp Wildcat on Wildcat Mountain.

OCTOBER 21, MISSOURI Union attempts to cross the Potomac River at Harrison's Island fail in the Battle of Ball's Bluff.

OCTOBER 21, MISSOURI The Union controls southeastern Missouri after the Battle of Fredericktown.

NOVEMBER 7, MISSOURI Ulysses S. Grant's Union forces defeat Confederates at the Battle of Belmont.

OTHER EVENTS

OCTOBER 22, UNITED STATES The first telegraph line is completed linking the east and west coasts.

NOVEMBER 1, UNITED STATES Jefferson Davis is elected as president of the Confederacy.

October

November

Ironclads had never before been used in combat when the Confederates converted a partly destroyed Union ship, the *Merrimack*. Engineers covered the vessel's hull with iron plating 4 inches (10 cm) thick. They also added a ram to its bow. Renamed CSS *Virginia*, the ship managed to sink two large Union warships and damage another in just a few hours in the Chesapeake Bay on March 8, 1862.

Ironclad vs ironclad

The next morning the *Virginia* returned to Hampton Roads. This time, however, the crew was astonished to be met by an enemy ironclad. This was the USS *Monitor*. Although it was smaller than the *Virginia*, it sat lower in the water and had a revolving gun turret. It was quicker, too, so it was able to outmaneuver the other ship as the two vessels pounded each other at close range for almost four hours. The running battle ended at dusk. The *Virginia* withdrew into safety of the James River. It had been hit 97 times over the two days. The *Monitor* had been hit 21 times. The armor was so effective, however, than neither vessel was badly damaged.

The battle had little immediate effect, but it showed how naval warfare was changing. Both sides rushed to build ironclads as quickly as possible. The Union's industrial production was far greater than that of the Confederacy, however, so it would win the final naval victory.

The CSS *Virginia* (right) exchanges fire with the USS *Monitor* during the Battle of Hampton Roads.

NOVEMBER 8, CUBA The British steamer *Trent* is stopped by Union warship *San Jacinto* in an action that breaks international law, as Britain is not a combatant in the Civil War.

NOVEMBER 8, KENTUCKY The Battle of Ivy Mountain, also known as Ivy Creek, sees Union soldiers push Confederates back into Virginia.

DECEMBER 20, VIRGINIA Union troops defeat Confederate cavalry under J.E.B. "Jeb" Stuart in the Battle of Dranesville.

NOVEMBER 19, UNITED STATES Julia Howe writes the first verses of "The Battle Hymn of the Republic."

DECEMBER 14, GREAT BRITAIN Prince Albert, the husband of Queen Victoria, dies, plunging his wife into a long period of mourning.

Battle of Shiloh

The second major battle of the Civil War was fought in the Western Theater on April 6–7, 1862. Both sides suffered heavy casualties as they clashed on the Tennessee River.

Troops of General Buell's Federal Army of the Ohio attack at the Battle of Shiloh on April 7.

The origins of the battle lay in the Union capture of Forts Henry and Donelson in February 1862. Those victories had opened the way for the Union forces of General Ulysses S. Grant to head south into Tennessee. Meanwhile the Confederate forces

1862
January–March

CIVIL WAR

JANUARY 18, ARIZONA
The Confederate Territory of Arizona is formed from part of what was the old Territory of New Mexico.

FEBRUARY 6, TENNESSEE
General Ulysses S. Grant takes the Confederate Fort Henry. The Tennessee River is now under Union control as far as Alabama.

FEBRUARY 16, TENNESSEE
Grant's troops take Fort Donelson; 15,000 Southerners surrender.

OTHER EVENTS

FEBRUARY, UNITED STATES
"The Battle Hymn of the Republic" is published and quickly becomes a popular marching song in the Union.

January   **February**

of Albert S. Johnston retreated before the Union advance.

By March the Union was moving two armies into position to advance. Grant's own army of 30,000 men moved to Pittsburg Landing on the Tennessee, 25 miles (40 km) north of Johnston's position at Corinth, Mississippi. Meanwhile Don Carlos Buell's even larger army—50,000 men— was about to leave Nashville, Tennessee, to join Grant.

This engraving shows intense hand-to-hand fighting in the Hornets' Nest at Shiloh.

Johnston believed that his best chance of recapturing western Tennessee and Nashville was to launch an offensive as quickly as possible. That way he might be able to defeat Grant before Buell arrived to reinforce him.

Taken by surprise

Johnston and his second in command, General Pierre G.T. Beauregard, gathered an army of 45,000 men. They set out for Pittsburg Landing on April 3, but the advance was badly organized and slowed down by bad weather. Johnston did not arrive south of Grant's position until the night of April 5.

Grant was unaware of Johnston's arrival. He had not set up lookouts to guard the army, so the Union soldiers had no idea that the enemy was near. The next morning, at about 5:00 A.M., thousands of men in gray charged out of the woods at the Union positions screaming the blood-curdling rebel yell.

FEBRUARY 25, TENNESSEE With the loss of forts Henry and Donelson, Nashville is the first Confederate state capital to fall to Union forces.

MARCH 6–8, ARKANSAS The Confederates are defeated at the Battle of Pea Ridge, the largest battle on Arkansas soil.

MARCH 8–9, VIRGINIA The Battle of Hampton Roads sees Confederate and Union ironclads fight to a standstill.

MARCH 17, VIRGINIA The Union Army of the Potomac sails to Fort Monroe to begin the Peninsular Campaign.

MARCH, EAST AFRICA Zanzibar becomes an independent nation.

MARCH 10, UNITED STATES The first U.S. paper money goes into circulation.

March

THE REBEL YELL

The famous Rebel Yell was first heard at Fort Donelson in February 1862. As they charged, Confederate troops made a blood-curdling, howling, whooping sound. Union troops said, "If you claim you heard it and you weren't scared, that means you never heard it."

The Confederates struck first at Shiloh Church, on the Union right, where they attacked William T. Sherman's division. They then struck the center of the line, where they pushed three divisions back. When Southern reinforcements arrived on the Union right, they helped force Sherman's men back to the Savannah Road by 10:00 A.M.

Meanwhile, the center and left of the Union line held firm in a peach orchard under Generals Hurlburt and Prentiss for nearly five hours. The noise of bullets buzzing through the air gave Prentiss's position the name "the Hornet's Nest." It saw some of the fiercest hand-to-hand fighting in the whole war.

By early afternoon three of Johnston's four corps were engaged in the battle. But the Union troops at the Peach Orchard and Hornet's Nest now threatened Johnston's own right flank, so he ordered his reserve corps forward. Shortly afterward, Johnston was shot and fatally wounded, and Beauregard took command.

Exhausted armies

Grant sent in reinforcements to help Sherman; Buell's divisions were also on their way. But the whole Union line was now dangerously close to collapse. In the center, Prentiss surrendered in the Hornets' Nest at about 5:30 P.M. Soldiers fled from the battlefield back down to Pittsburg Landing. Now Beauregard missed his chance. If he had pressed home his advantage, he might have had the chance to push Grant's army back into the river. But

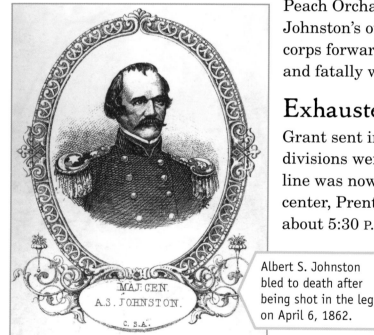

MAJ. GEN.
A.S. JOHNSTON.
C.S.A.

Albert S. Johnston bled to death after being shot in the leg on April 6, 1862.

1862 April–June

CIVIL WAR

APRIL 6–7, TENNESSEE In the Battle of Shiloh Ulysses S. Grant narrowly defeats Confederate forces, with heavy losses on both sides.

APRIL 12, GEORGIA Union agent James Ambrose steals a Confederate train on the Western & Atlantic Railroad. He is captured and hanged.

APRIL 29, THE SOUTH The Confederacy passes a conscription act forcing men aged 18 to 50 to enlist in the army; many farms go into decline as farmers join up.

APRIL 29, LOUISIANA The Union occupation of New Orleans opens access to the rest of Louisiana and the Mississippi Valley.

OTHER EVENTS

APRIL 8, UNITED STATES Inventor John D. Lynde patents the first aerosol spray.

April

Beauregard did not take the opportunity. Like their enemy, his own troops were exhausted after 14 hours of fierce fighting. At 7:00 P.M. the battlefield fell silent. Both sides decided to rest and prepare to resume the conflict in the morning.

The second day

Overnight, Grant stabilized his army. He reinforced it with Buell's divisions and concentrated his artillery above Pittsburg Landing. Early the next day, the Union troops counterattacked. The Confederates quickly lost all the ground they had won on the first day. At the end of the afternoon, General Beauregard ordered a general retreat to Corinth.

The battle was one of the bloodiest of the war. The South lost 10,700 killed and wounded for no gain. The North suffered 13,000 casualties, but only narrowly avoided defeat.

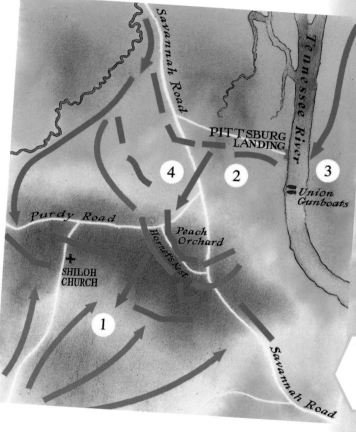

This map shows the positions of the two armies over the two days of the battle.

BATTLE DETAILS

1. The surprise Confederate attack early on April 6 drove the enemy back at Shiloh Church but met resistance at the "Hornet's Nest." After General Johnston was killed, Beauregard took over.

2. Confederates pushed Union troops back to the river by nightfall.

3. Buell arrived overnight with Union reinforcements.

4. Buell counterattacked on April 7. After a day's fighting, Beauregard ordered Confederate forces to withdraw to Corinth.

MAY 31, VIRGINIA
The Battle of Fair Oaks (Seven Pines) is drawn. Union losses are 5,050 and Confederate losses are 6,150.

JUNE 1, VIRGINIA
General Robert E. Lee takes command of the Army of Northern Virgina after General Joseph Johnston is wounded.

JUNE 12, VIRGINIA
J.E.B. Stuart and 1,200 cavalry raid the Union camp outside Richmond, taking 165 prisoners.

JUNE 25, VIRGINIA
The first battle of the Seven Days' Campaign—the Battle of Oak Grove—sees McClellan's Union forces halted near Richmond.

MAY 5, MEXICO
A Mexican army defeats an invading French force in the Battle of Puebla.

MAY 20, UNITED STATES
The Homestead Act makes millions of acres of Western land available to settlers.

Fall of New Orleans

The capture of New Orleans, Louisiana, was a major Union war aim. It would give the Union control of the Mississippi Delta, while the Confederacy would lose its busiest port and banking center.

Union sailors in a rowboat confront an angry crowd in New Orleans on April 25, 1862.

New Orleans was not a typical Southern city. Its 1860 population of 170,000 was far more ethnically diverse than most other places in the South. This reflected the city's history of colonial occupation. Many people were of French and Spanish

1862 July–September

CIVIL WAR

JULY 1, WASHINGTON, D.C. The Union introduces an Internal Revenue Act, imposing a tax on income to raise money to pay for the war.

JULY 13, WASHINGTON, D.C. President Lincoln reads a draft of the Emancipation Proclamation to his cabinet.

JULY 17, THE NORTH The Confiscation Act and Militia Act come into force, opening the way for the creation of black regiments of freed slaves.

AUGUST 29, VIRGINIA The Second Battle of Bull Run (Manassas) begins.

OTHER EVENTS

JULY 4, GREAT BRITAIN Lewis Carroll makes up the story that will become Alice in Wonderland to amuse a young friend.

JULY 14, UNITED STATES Congress introduces the Medal of Honor for valor in the military services.

July

August

ancestry. The city was home to a mixture of free blacks, white Southerners, and businesspeople from the North. Immigrants from Europe made up over a third of the population. One result of such diversity was that secession was not as popular in New Orleans as in other parts of the South. New Orleans voted to leave the Union by only 52 to 48 percent.

The Louisiana authorities posted few soldiers in New Orleans. They believed that the city was protected from any Union attack by Forts Jackson and St. Philip, which stood on the Mississippi River 75 miles (120 km) south of the city. They were wrong. In April 1862, a fleet of 17 Union gunboats sailed up the river and bombarded the forts into surrender. New Orleans fell on April 29. The rest of Louisiana and the Mississippi Valley now lay open to Union advances.

An infamous order

The occupying forces in New Orleans were commanded by Major General Benjamin F. Butler. In order to prevent women harassing Union soldiers, Butler issued his infamous Order 28, or "Woman's Order." Southerners were outraged by Butler's decree that women who insulted Union troops would be imprisoned as prostitutes. They nicknamed him "Beast" Butler, and his actions became a rallying call throughout the Confederacy. Butler also made history by allowing free blacks to form a military regiment, the "Corps d'Afrique." After only seven months Butler was replaced by the far less controversial Major General Nathaniel P. Banks. Union occupation of New Orleans only ended in March 1866.

A poster calls on people in New Orleans to protest against Union General Benjamin Butler's Order 28, the infamous "Woman's Order."

AUGUST 30, VIRGINIA
Confederate Robert E. Lee defeats the Union army at Bull Run. His casualties stand at 9,500, while Union losses are 14,500.

SEPTEMBER 17, MARYLAND
The Battle of Antietam ends in a draw after heavy losses on both sides: Lee's Army of Northern Virginia suffers 10,000 casualties; the Union Army of the Potomac loses 12,400 dead, wounded, or missing.

SEPTEMBER 22, WASHINGTON, D.C.
Lincoln issues a preliminary Emancipation Proclamation.

SEPTEMBER 24, TENNESSEE
Union General William Sherman orders the destruction of every house in Randolph in revenge for Confederate shelling of his steamboats.

AUGUST 18, MINNESOTA
An uprising by young Sioux Indians leaves more than 800 white settlers dead.

Advance on Richmond

In March 1862 the Union began the Peninsular Campaign. General George B. McClellan planned to attack the Confederate capital from the east, across the Virginia Peninsula.

Union cavalry water their horses while gunboats fire on enemy positions at the Battle of Malvern Hill, Virginia.

The plan for the campaign was McClellan's own. The Union commander-in-chief, President Abraham Lincoln, had preferred an offensive that would have driven from Washington, D.C., straight toward Richmond through northern Virginia.

1862
October–December

CIVIL WAR

OCTOBER 3, MISSISSIPPI
A Union army defeats the Confederates in the Battle of Corinth.

OCTOBER 11, VIRGINIA
The Confederate Congress passes an unpopular draft law that exempts anyone owning more than 20 slaves—the wealthiest part of society—from military service.

NOVEMBER 7, WASHINGTON, D.C.
Lincoln fires George B. McClellan as commander of the Army of the Potomac and appoints Ambrose E. Burnside in his place.

OTHER EVENTS

OCTOBER 8, PRUSSIA Otto von Bismarck becomes minister-president of Prussia; he uses his position to mastermind the unification of Germany.

NOVEMBER 4, UNITED STATES
Richard Gatling patents the machine gun that is named for him: the Gatling gun.

October   November

McClellan, the commander of the Army of the Potomac, wanted to exploit the Union navy's control of the coast. He could ship troops from Washington via the Potomac River to Fort Monroe, a Union-held stronghold on the Virginia Peninsula. From there, it was only 75 miles (120 km) to Richmond. McClellan anticipated that enemy opposition on the peninsula would be light, while the Union forces could be kept supplied by sea.

The Union army's supply base at White House Landing was the target of General Robert E. Lee.

Lincoln reluctantly agreed to McClellan's plan. He was alarmed by reports that Confederate General "Stonewall" Jackson was active in the Shenandoah Valley. Lincoln was anxious that McClellan would not leave enough troops to defend Washington if Jackson advanced. Lincoln withdrew a whole corps from McClellan's command to remain in northern Virginia to protect the capital. This began a breakdown in the relationship between the president and his commander that would badly reflect the campaign.

A hesitant advance

The Union operation began smoothly. By April 1 McClellan had 100 guns and was assembling an army that would eventually total 100,000 men. The Confederate reaction was highly effective, however. General John B. Magruder hastily built two defensive lines between the York and the James rivers. He also

DECEMBER 7, TENNESSEE
Confederates defeat Union troops at the Battle of Hartsville, opening parts of western Tennessee and Kentucky.

DECEMBER 13–14, VIRGINIA
Burnside is beaten back in the Battle of Fredericksburg, with the loss of 6,500 Union troops.

DECEMBER 31, TENNESSEE
Union troops triumph in the Battle of Murfreesboro, taking Kentucky and increasing their hold on Tennessee.

DECEMBER 30, UNITED STATES
Lincoln reads his Emancipation Proclamation to his cabinet for comments.

DECEMBER 31, UNITED STATES
Lincoln signs an act admitting West Virginia to the Union.

Map showing the progress of the Union Army of the Potomac up the Virginia Peninsula toward Richmond.

THE ARMY OF THE POTOMAC

Created in August 1861, the Army of the Potomac was the Union's main field force in the eastern theater. It was usually the Union's largest army at any time, with an average strength of about 120,000 men. It lost almost every major battle it fought.

succeeded in fooling McClellan into believing that his force of 13,000 was much larger than it was. Faced with Magruder's defenses at Yorktown, McClellan became convinced he faced an army of at least 100,000. Instead of sweeping Magruder aside and racing for Richmond, he hesitated and laid siege to Yorktown.

Lincoln sent urgent telegrams telling McClellan to advance. Instead, McClellan delayed at Yorktown for a month while the Confederate commander on the peninsula, Joseph E. Johnston, gathered reinforcements. He placed some 75,000 defenders along the Chickahominy River, a few miles east of Richmond, then ordered Magruder to fall back from Yorktown. At last McClellan began to advance.

A new Confederate hero

By the end of May the armies were around the villages of Fair Oaks and Seven Pines, near the Chickahominy. McClellan's army was split. He had 60,000 men north of the river and 31,500 to the south.

On May 31, Johnston attacked McClellan's southern wing in the Battle of Fair Oaks (Seven Pines). Both sides suffered heavy losses, but the most important casualty was Johnston,

1863
January–March

CIVIL WAR

JANUARY 1, WASHINGTON, D.C.
The Emancipation Proclamation comes into effect, ruling that slaves in the South are free. The Civil War is now a war for the abolition of slavery, as well as a struggle to preserve the Union.

JANUARY 20–22, VIRGINIA
The Union Army of the Potomac tries to cross the Rappahannock River but turns back as rain turns the ground to mud.

OTHER EVENTS

JANUARY 1, WASHINGTON, D.C.
The Homestead Act comes into law, encouraging western migration by granting land to farmers.

JANUARY 10, GREAT BRITAIN
The world's first underground railroad line opens in London.

FEBRUARY 3, UNITED STATES
Newspaper editor Samuel Clemens first uses the pen name by which he will become famous: Mark Twain.

January   **February**

who was badly wounded. On June 1 General Robert E. Lee took command of the Army of Northern Virginia. For two weeks of pouring rain, both sides strengthened their positions.

The Seven Days' Campaign

On June 12, Lee sent the South's outstanding cavalry commander, J.E.B. Stuart, to gather information about McClellan. Stuart and his 1,200 men made a famous three-day ride that carried them around the whole Union army. Stuart learned that four of McClellan's corps were now south of the river. There was just one corps on the north bank, protecting a Union supply base near Mechanicsville, at White House Landing on the Pamunkey River.

Such a weak target was what Lee was looking for. He attacked McClellan's lone corps on June 26, and forced it back south of the river. With Lee also attacking his left flank, McClellan abandoned his offensive. On the 27th he ordered his forces to retreat south. The Battle of Mechanicsville was the first of what became known as the Seven Days' Campaign: a series of Union rearguard actions that frustrated Lee's attempts to deliver a killer blow. By July 2 McClellan's army was back at Harrison's Landing—the Peninsular Campaign had failed.

Union engineers lay a "corduroy road" of logs to enable artillery and heavy supply wagons to pass over soft ground.

RIVER WAR

The York and James rivers were crucial in the Peninsular Campaign. Typically, they helped the Confederate army form their defensive lines while they provided an obstacle for the Union army. McClellan used river transports and gunboats to establish his base close to Richmond. When he retreated to Harrison's Landing on the James River, gunboats sheltered his withdrawal.

FEBRUARY 24, UNITED STATES
Arizona is organized as a territory of the United States.

MARCH 3, UNITED STATES
The territory of Idaho is created.

MARCH 3, WASHINGTON, D.C.
The Union introduces the National Conscription Act, obliging men to join the army or pay $300 to hire a substitute.

MARCH 3, THE SOUTH
The Confederacy introduces an unpopular Impressment Act that allows army officers to take food from farmers at set rates.

Battle of Fair Oaks (Seven Pines)

By the end of May 1862, the Pensinular Campaign had brought the Union Army of the Potomac to the outskirts of the Confederate capital at Richmond, Virginia.

Union soldiers bury their dead comrades and burn the dead horses after the battle.

In McClellan's way stood the Confederate Army of Northern Virginia, commanded by General Joseph E. Johnston. McClellan's delays in advancing up the Virginia peninsula had given Johnston time to reinforce his defenses, positioned on the

1863
April–June

CIVIL WAR

APRIL 2, VIRGINIA "Bread riots" break out in the Confederacy over the high price of food; the worst riots are in Richmond.

APRIL 17, MISSISSIPPI Union cavalry raids Mississippi, tearing up railroad lines. Soldiers ride south to the Union city of Baton Rouge, Louisiana.

MAY 2–4, VIRGINIA The Confederate Army of Northern Virginia defeats the Union Army of the Potomac at the Battle of Chancellorsville; however, Confederate commander "Stonewall" Jackson is shot by one of his own men and dies.

MAY 14, MISSISSIPPI Union troops capture Jackson, the fourth state capital to fall to Union troops.

OTHER EVENTS

MAY 22, UNITED STATES The War Department establishes the Bureau of Colored Troops.

April   May

Chickahominy River just outside Richmond. McClellan decided to split his army, sending part of it to join an advance from Fredericksburg.

The division of the Union army gave Johnston a chance to strike. He had 75,000 troops available, while the two Union corps south of the river had only 31,500 troops under generals Erasmus D. Keyes and Samuel P. Heintzelman.

Confederates prepare to face a Union bayonet charge during the battle.

Inconclusive clash

Johnston decided to exploit his strength by advancing along three roads that all met at Keyes' position at Seven Pines. However, he gave his orders orally rather than writing them down. As they maneuvered on May 31, his troops' movements became confused, especially because rain had turned the ground into clogging mud.

Six hours after the attack should have begun, only six of 13 Confederate brigades were in position. But a determined assault pushed back McClellan's men to a third defensive line by evening. At about 7:00 P.M. Johnston was seriously wounded, and command passed to General Gustavus W. Smith.

The next day Smith launched another attack before he was replaced. His replacement ordered a general withdrawal. The battle had no clear outcome. More significant was the man President Jefferson Davis had chosen as the new commander of the Army of Northern Virginia: General Robert E. Lee.

MAY 18, MISSISSIPPI
Union armies begin the siege of Vicksburg.

JUNE 9, VIRGINIA
The Battle of Brandy Station ends in a Confederate victory.

JUNE 14, VIRGINIA
The Battle of Winchester is another Confederate victory.

JUNE 16, VIRGINIA
Lee orders the Army of Northern Virginia across the Potomac River to invade the North for a second time.

JUNE 28, WASHINGTON, D.C.
Lincoln replaces General Joseph Hooker as commander of the Army of the Potomac with General George Meade, whom he hopes will be more aggressive.

JUNE 7, MEXICO French troops capture Mexico City; the French want to begin a colony while Americans are distracted by the war.

JUNE 20, UNITED STATES
West Virginia is admitted to the Union following a presidential proclamation.

Seven Days' Campaign

After the Confederates halted McClellan's Peninsular Campaign outside Richmond, Virginia, the Union found itself fighting a desperate retreat to avoid a decisive defeat by Robert E. Lee.

Union artillery in action at the Battle of Malvern Hill, Virginia, fought on July 1, 1862.

In the spring of 1862 the Union General George B. McClellan had led more than 100,000 men of the Army of the Potomac across the Virginia Peninsula in an attempt to capture Richmond, the Confederate capital. At the end of May

1863 July–September

CIVIL WAR

JULY 1–3, PENNSYLVANNIA
The Battle of Gettysburg yields more than 20,000 casualties on each side in a decisive Union victory that marks a turning point in the war.

JULY 4, MISSISSIPPI
The fall of Vicksburg to the Union splits the Confederacy in two.

JULY 13, NEW YORK
Antidraft riots erupt across the North; in the worst, in New York City, African Americans are attacked and draft offices burned.

JULY 18, SOUTH CAROLINA
The 54th Massachusetts Volunteer Infantry, a black Union unit, fails in a courageous attack on Fort Wagner.

OTHER EVENTS

JULY 1, SOUTH AMERICA
The Dutch abolish slavery in their colony in Suriname.

JULY, CAMBODIA French writers reveal for the first time the existence of the remarkable ruined city of Angkor in the Cambodian jungle.

July

McClellan's army was at Seven Pines, only 10 miles (16 km) from Richmond. Joseph E. Johnston's Army of Northern Virginia attacked McClellan on May 31, but it failed to dislodge him. Johnston himself was seriously wounded during the battle. He was replaced by Robert E. Lee.

Battle of Mechanicsville

As Lee strengthened the city's defenses and planned an attack, he sent J.E.B. Stuart's cavalry to try to locate the northern flank of the Union army. Stuart rode right around McClellan's force, and found that it was split on either side of the Chickahominy River. McClellan had left only one corps on the north bank of the river near Mechanicsville to defend the Union supply base at White House Landing. This corps was Lee's first objective.

On June 17 Lee began to reinforce his army to go on the offensive. He ordered General Thomas "Stonewall" Jackson to

This contemporary drawing shows a division of the Army of the Potomac led by George A. McCall.

AUGUST 17, SOUTH CAROLINA Union forces begin a bombardment of Fort Sumter in Charleston Harbor, the place where the first shots of the war were fired.

AUGUST 20, KANSAS William Quantrill's Confederate guerrillas attack Lawrence, killing more than 150 civilians and destroying 200 buildings.

SEPTEMBER 19–20, TENNESSEE Confederates win a hollow victory at the two-day Battle of Chickamauga, losing 18,000 to the Union's 16,000, and forcing only a partial Union withdrawal to Chattanooga.

SEPTEMBER 29, ITALY Troops led by the nationalist Giuseppe Garibaldi defeat a papal army, a major obstruction to Italian unification.

RICHMOND

At the start of the Civil War, Richmond, Virginia—100 miles (160 km) from Washington, D.C.—was a prosperous city and the South's main manufacturing center. It was the Confederate capital for most of the war. By the war's end, it was almost completely destroyed.

bring his army from from the Shenandoah Valley, which would bring Lee's strength up to about 87,000 men. Jackson promised to arrive on June 25. Lee planned to attack the following day.

Seven Days' Campaign

The Battle of Mechanicsville on June 26 was the first of the Seven Days' Campaign. Lee's initial attack across the Chickahominy pushed back the Union right but then faltered. Jackson arrived too late to enable Lee to strike a decisive blow. The Union army was now on the defensive, however. McClellan held a line at Beaver Dam Creek, but with typical caution, he ordered a withdrawal to Gaines' Mill. There he again came under attack from Lee on the 27th. This time McClellan withdrew his army south across the Chickahominy. The Union commander began to lose his nerve. The siege of Richmond was no longer possible. Instead, his priority was to try to save his army. He ordered his entire force back to take up defensive positions on the James River.

Lee pursued his retreating enemy and kept up the offensive, but he proved unable to deliver a decisive blow. On June 29 the Army of the Potomac held off a Confederate attack at Savage's

Union forces fought during the retreat south to the James River.

1863
October–December

CIVIL WAR

OCTOBER 15, SOUTH CAROLINA
Confederate submarine *H.L. Hunley* sinks on its second test voyage, drowning all its crew.

NOVEMBER 19, PENNSYLVANIA
Lincoln makes his famous "Gettysburg Address" during the dedication of the cemetery on the battlefield.

OTHER EVENTS

OCTOBER 3, UNITED STATES
President Abraham Lincoln proclaims the last Thursday in November as Thanksgiving Day.

OCTOBER 23, SWITZERLAND
The first conference of the International Committee of the Red Cross is held.

NOVEMBER 23, UNITED STATES
A patent is granted to the first process for color photography.

October   November

An eyewitness drawing of fighting near Mechanicsville.

Station. The next day it withdrew through Frayser's Farm (Glendale). Here Lee was again thwarted. His army's advance was bogged down in White Oak Swamp. In the difficult terrain, his divisions failed to coordinate their attacks well enough to prevent Union troops from retreating again.

End of the campaign

Lee got his last chance to stop McClellan at Malvern Hill on July 1. Knowing that McClellan was within reach of safety, Lee tried to win a decisive victory. He made a series of frontal assaults on the Union position, but the infantry was met by barrages from more than 100 Union cannons. The Confederate artillery could not match such firepower. The Army of Northern Virginia was exhausted. Lee gave up his pursuit.

On July 2 the Army of the Potomac reached Harrison's Landing on the James River. Four weeks later, it sailed from there to return north. Lee had saved Richmond, but at a high cost. In only a week, he had lost a quarter of his army—more than 20,000 men. For his part, McClellan had missed his chance to take Richmond. Union forces would not be so close to the Confederate capital again for another two years.

AN UNAMBITIOUS HERO

General George B. McClellan (1826–1885) rose quickly to take command of the Union army. He created an effective fighting force from raw recruits, but his lack of decisiveness made him a poor battlefield commander. McClellan's ambition and the Union rout at First Bull Run saw him rise in a few months to command of the entire Union Army. He established the Army of the Potomac, but it was not until April 1862 that Lincoln could persuade him to send out his army to fight. On the battlefield, he proved unfit for command. McClellan made many mistakes throughout the Peninsular Campaign, and his failures at the Second Battle of Bull Run and Antietam proved his undoing.

NOVEMBER 23, TENNESSEE
The Battle of Chattanooga sees Union troops push back the Confederates.

NOVEMBER 24–25, TENNESSEE The Union capture of Chattanooga opens the "Gateway to the South."

DECEMBER 1, WASHINGTON, D.C.
Confederate spy Belle Boyd is freed from prison by Union authorities.

DECEMBER 9, TENNESSEE
After a 16-day siege, Confederate defenders withdraw from the town of Knoxville.

DECEMBER 16, TENNESSEE General Joseph Johnston takes command of the Confederate Army of Tennessee, replacing General William Hardee.

NOVEMBER 26, UNITED STATES
The first modern Thanksgiving Day is celebrated in the North.

DECEMBER 1, CHILE
A fire in a church causes panic in which 1,500 worshipers die.

Battle of Gaines' Mill

Gaines' Mill was the second and the most decisive engagement of the Seven Days' Campaign in Virginia. It was Confederate commander Robert E. Lee's first victory of the Civil War.

Union forces destroy a bridge over the Chickahominy River using a train loaded with ammunition.

Lee had only recently taken over as the commander of the main Confederate army, the Army of Northern Virginia. He decided that the best way to defend the capital at Richmond was to go on the offensive. On June 26 he attacked

1864
January–March

CIVIL WAR

JANUARY 14, GEORGIA Union General William T. Sherman begins his infamous March through the South.

JANUARY 17, TENNESSEE At the Battle of Dandridge, Confederate forces repel Union troops from the Dandridge area.

FEBRUARY 9, VIRGINIA A total of 109 Union prisoners escape through a tunnel at Libby Prison in Richmond.

FEBRUARY 14–20, MISSISSIPPI In the Battle of Meridian, William T. Sherman leads a successful Union raid to destroy an important railroad junction.

OTHER EVENTS

FEBRUARY 1, DENMARK Prussian forces invade the Danish province of Schleswig, beginning the Second Schleswig War.

January

February

the right flank of the Army of the Potomac at Mechanicsville, where a Union corps was split from the rest of the army by the Chickahominy River. Lee's subordinates bungled the attack, but the battle did force General George B. McClellan to begin withdrawing south from Richmond toward to the James River.

At Gaines' Mill

As the Union army withdrew, its rear was defended by V Corps. On June 27, the corps took up a strong defensive position on high ground near Boatswain's Creek, a tributary of the Chickahominy. The troops were positioned between the village of Cold Harbor and Mr. Gaines' farm and mill, which gave the battle its name.

Lee's forces had now been joined by the corps of Thomas J. "Stonewall" Jackson, including the Texas Brigade led by John Bell Hood. As at Mechanicsville, however, Lee and his officers had problems coordinating their assaults. Several attacks failed until near sunset, when a frontal attack by the Texans broke through the Union line. At nightfall V Corps joined in the general Union withdrawal. At a cost of 8,750 casualties Lee had earned his first battlefield victory of the Civil War. The battle also cemented the reputation of Hood's Texas Brigade as a successful battlefield unit.

Defeat at Gaines' Mill forced McClellan to abandon his advance on Richmond.

FEBRUARY 20, FLORIDA Many men of the 8th Regiment of United States Colored Troops are killed or injured in the Battle of Olustee near Jacksonville; Union forces retreat to the coast.

MARCH 2, THE NORTH Lieutenant General Ulysees S. Grant is made commander of all the armies of the United States.

MARCH 25, KENTUCKY Confederate cavalry attack the city of Paducah on the Ohio River; they retreat the next day, having suffered many casualties.

MARCH 14, AFRICA British explorers Samuel and Florence Baker discover Lake Albert at the headwaters of the Nile River.

Second Bull Run (Manassas)

As its name suggests, the Second Battle of Bull Run was fought over the same ground as the first battle just over a year earlier. The second battle was an outstanding victory for Robert E. Lee.

This house on Henry Hill was left in ruins after the two battles at Bull Run.

Lee's plan for the battle was risky. In June 1862 he had defeated the Union's first advance on Richmond, but now he found his Army of Northern Virginia sandwiched between two larger Union armies. The new Army of Virginia, led by General

1864
April–June

CIVIL WAR

APRIL 12, TENNESSEE Confederate troops massacre the Union garrison at Fort Pillow, killing 202 African Americans.

APRIL 17, GEORGIA Hungry citizens of Savannah stage bread riots over the lack of food.

MAY 3, VIRGINIA The Union Army of the Potomac starts to move south, crossing the difficult terrain of the Wilderness region.

OTHER EVENTS

APRIL 10, MEXICO The French declare Archuduke Maximilian of Austria to be emperor of Mexico.

APRIL 22, UNITED STATES Congress decides to print the phrase "In God We Trust" on U.S. coins.

MAY 9, NORTH SEA Austria and Denmark fight a naval battle at Heligoland during the Second Schleswig War.

April

May

John Pope, was advancing from the north. On the other side, the Army of the Potomac was preparing for another campaign.

Lee wanted to defeat Pope before he could be reinforced by the Army of the Potomac. Against conventional military wisdom, he twice divided his forces. He sent "Stonewall" Jackson to fight Pope in central Virginia and then sent Jackson and James Longstreet on a 60-mile (96-km) march to outflank Pope and cut his supply lines. The Confederates then reunited at Manassas.

Confederate troops at the captured Union supply depot at Manassas Junction on August 26, 1862.

A complete victory

Union forces attacked the Confederate positions on August 29. The defenders ran so low on ammunition that some had to throw stones at the enemy. The Union attacks were poorly coordinated, however, and the Confederate line held until nightfall. The next day brought more attacks. Pope had neglected his left flank, however, and it was crushed by a Confederate counterattack. Pope and his beaten army retreated to the fortifications around Washington.

Second Bull Run was the most complete of Robert E. Lee's victories. The Union advance on Richmond was defeated. Lee had inflicted 14,500 casualties on the enemy, but suffered only 9,500 himself. Lee now felt able to take the initiative: He would invade the North and win another decisive victory there.

MAY 5–6, VIRGINIA
Grant and Lee fight the inconclusive Battle of the Wilderness.

MAY 12, VIRGINIA
Grant and Lee fight again at the Battle of Spotsylvania. The battle is a draw.

JUNE 3, VIRGINIA
The Battle of Cold Harbor is a disaster for the Union army. They lose 7,000 men for no gain against Confederate losses of 1,500.

JUNE 27, GEORGIA
The Battle of Kennesaw Mountain sees Sherman's Union troops suffer heavy losses of 3,000 against Johnston's Confederate troops losses of 552.

MAY, GREAT BRITAIN
Charles Dickens publishes the first part of *Our Mutual Friend*.

MAY 26, UNITED STATES
Congress creates the territory of Montana, with its original capital at Virginia City.

JUNE 15, UNITED STATES Secretary of War Edwin M. Stanton creates Arlington National Cemetery, Virginia, on land previously owned by Confederate General Robert E. Lee.

Battle of South Mountain

Early in September 1862, Robert E. Lee led the Army of Northern
Virginia across the Potomac River into Maryland.
The main army of the Confederacy was on Northern soil.

This painting shows a Union charge during the Battle of South Mountain.

The Union commander, General George B. McClellan,
received intelligence that Lee had split his forces. McClellan
planned to attack part of the Southern army before it was able
to join back together. He led the Army of the Potomac out from

1864
July–September

CIVIL WAR

JULY 9, MARYLAND
Confederates defeat
Union troops at the
Battle of Monocacy.

**JULY 11,
WASHINGTON, D.C.**
Facing strong Union
defenses, Confederates
withdraw from their
attack.

JULY 22, GEORGIA
Confederate General
Hood's troops fail to
defeat General Sherman's
men at the Battle of
Atlanta. Confederate
losses are 8,000; Union
losses are 3,600.

AUGUST 5, ALABAMA Union
warships defeat Confederate
vessels at the Battle of Mobile
Bay: Union admiral David G.
Farragut is said to have
ordered, "Damn the torpedoes;
full speed ahead!"

**OTHER
EVENTS**

JULY 5, UNITED STATES The
Bank of California is founded
with holdings of $2 million.

JULY 14, UNITED STATES
Gold is discovered in Montana
at Helena, which will later
become the state capital.

AUGUST 8, SWITZERLAND
The first Geneva Convention is
held to discuss the treatment
of wounded soldiers in war.

July   August

Washington, D.C., into Maryland. McClellan planned to cross the Blue Ridge Mountains that divided the state through three passes near South Mountain: Crampton's Gap, Fox's Gap, and Turner's Gap. Once on the other side of the mountain, he would be able to engage Lee's army.

Blocking the passes

Lee had been warned that McClellan knew his plans. While he began to gather his army at Sharpsburg (Antietam), he sent a small division east under Daniel H. Hill to defend a ridge along South Mountain and prevent McClellan's pursuit.

Early on September 14, McClellan's corps commanders got their men into position for the attack. At Crampton's Gap, VI Corps easily overcame a thin Confederate defensive line but were held up by a stronger counterattack. The story was similar at Fox's and Turner's Gaps: Hill's brigades blocked the passes for the whole day. They were helped by the Union tactics. General Ambrose E. Burnside sent troops into battle little by little, allowing Hill time to move his men and reinforcements where they were needed. It was only at nightfall that Union troops opened Crampton's and Fox's Gaps; Turner's Gap was not cleared until dawn on September 15.

Hill had held up the Union army for a whole day. That was crucial in allowing Lee to prepare for the bloody battle that was to come.

A Union 10-pounder Parrott cannon about to be fired during a training exercise.

AUGUST 31, ILLINOIS The Democratic National Convention in Chicago nominates General George B. McClellan as its presidential candidate on an antiwar ticket.

SEPTEMBER 1, GEORGIA General Sherman cuts the last supply line to Atlanta, the railroad, forcing the Confederates to leave the city.

SEPTEMBER 16, VIRGINIA Confederate cavalrymen raid Union beef supplies on the James River to feed hungry Southerners.

SEPTEMBER 22, VIRGINIA Union forces defeat Confederates at the Battle of Fisher's Hill and start to destroy crops in the Shenandoah Valley.

SEPTEMBER 5, JAPAN British, Dutch, and French fleets attack Japan to open the Shimonoseki Straits to navigation.

SEPTEMBER 15, ITALY The new country gives up its claims to Rome; the Italians agree to make Florence their capital.

Battle of Antietam (Sharpsburg)

On September 17, 1862, the Army of Northern Virginia and the Army of the Potomac clashed in Maryland in the bloodiest single day of the Civil War: around 23,000 men were killed or wounded.

The Union forces attacked from the north and east, but delays limited their effectiveness.

The battle was the climax of Confederate Robert E. Lee's first invasion of the North. Lee believed that his army was in a strong position, having already defeated two separate Union armies in recent months. He knew that there was little to be

1864
October–November

CIVIL WAR

OCTOBER 19, VIRGINIA
Union forces, under General Sheridan, defeat Jubal Early's Confederate Army of the Valley at the Battle of Cedar Creek.

OCTOBER 26, ALABAMA
Union forces at Decatur prevent Confederates led by John Bell Hood from crossing the Tennessee River in an attempt to cut William T. Sherman's lines of communication.

OCTOBER 27, VIRGINIA
Union forces assaulting the Confederate capital at Richmond are defeated in the Second Battle of Fair Oaks.

OTHER EVENTS

OCTOBER 11, UNITED STATES
Slavery is abolished in Maryland.

OCTOBER 30, AUSTRIA The Peace of Vienna ends the Second Schleswig War between Germany and Denmark.

OCTOBER 31, UNITED STATES
Nevada is admitted to the Union as the 36th state.

October

gained by attacking Washington, D.C., which was strongly defended. Instead, he invaded Maryland on September 4, 1862. A few days later, he split his forces. His trusted General Thomas "Stonewall" Jackson led half of the army west, where they captured Harpers Ferry, West Virginia.

Concentrating the army

Facing Lee was General George B. McClellan and the Army of the Potomac. On September 13 Union troops captured a copy of Lee's orders. McClellan learned that the Confederates were divided and marched north, between the two halves of the army.

This contemporary photograph shows the small town of Sharpsburg, scene of the war's bloodiest day.

Lee decided to concentrate his troops near the town of Sharpsburg, between the Potomac and Antietam Creek. He ordered Jackson to join him there. By September 16 Lee was in position on high ground above Sharpsburg. His 18,000 men were arranged along a 3-mile (4.5-km) line on either side of the Boonsboro Pike. The troops were exposed, with little natural cover and no way of retreat apart from a ford across the Potomac River behind them. Jackson had not yet arrived. The Confederates faced an army more than three times bigger: over 75,000 men, moving from the north and east.

The fighting begins

Fighting began at dusk on September 16. Union troops under Joseph Hooker began attacking from the north. By now, however, the first of Jackson's units had begun to arrive.

NOVEMBER 4, TENNESSEE
Confederate cavalry commander Nathan B. Forrest completes a 23-day raid in Georgia and Tennessee by destroying a Union supply base at Johsonville.

NOVEMBER 15, GEORGIA
Union general William T. Sherman burns much of Atlanta before setting out on his notorious "March to the Sea."

NOVEMBER 25, NEW YORK
Confederate spies fail in a plot to burn down New York City.

NOVEMBER 8, UNITED STATES
Abraham Lincoln is reelected for a second term as president of the United States.

NOVEMBER 29, UNITED STATES
Militia in Colorado massacre some 200 Cheyenne and Arapaho at Sand Creek in retaliation for an attack on settlers.

A Union signal tower on Elk Mountain overlooks the battlefield.

BLOODIEST DAY

September 17, 1862, at Antietam was the bloodiest day of the entire Civil War. The Union suffered losses of 12,400 dead, wounded, or missing while the Confederate losses stood at more than 10,000 men.

Reinforced, the Confederates had repulsed the advance by the time darkness fell.

At 6:00 A.M. on September 17, McClellan began the day's battle with an artillery bombardment. Hooker's I Corps attacked again. He sent ten brigades against the Confederate left, and pushed them back to the West Woods. Jackson counterattacked at 7:00 A.M., but another Union corps reinforced Hooker.

A fierce battle raged in the West Woods for the possession of the Dunker Church. Three more divisions advanced from the Union right to join the fighting. As they charged into the West Woods, however, General John Sedgewick's division advanced straight into a Confederate line. Only 20 minutes later, more than 2,500 of the division were dead or wounded. Sedgwick himself was wounded three times. The Union troops fell back to take up defensive positions. The fighting for the West Woods was at a stalemate.

Bloody Lane

Some of the heaviest fighting took place at "Bloody Lane," the name later given to a sunken road between the Boonsboro and Haegerstown Pikes. Having lost its way, a Union division blundered into Confederate brigades there at 9:30 A.M. Lee sent in reserves to help defend the position, and fighting raged for nearly four hours before the Union finally won control.

The Confederate line was now in grave danger. On its right the Union IX Corps, commanded by Ambrose E. Burnside, had

1864–1865
December–January

CIVIL WAR

DECEMBER 13, GEORGIA
Union troops capture Fort McAllister near Savannah.

DECEMBER 15, TENNESSEE
At the Battle of Nashville, the Confederate Army of Tennessee is defeated by the Union Army of the Cumberland.

DECEMBER 20, GEORGIA
The Confederate garrison escapes from Savannah.

DECEMBER 21, GEORGIA
Sherman and his men enter Savannah unopposed at the conclusion of the March to the Sea.

OTHER EVENTS

DECEMBER 8, VATICAN Pope Pius IX publishes the Syllabus of Errors, which condemns liberalism and reformism.

December

been attacking across Antietam Creek at the Rohrbach Bridge. Just as Bloody Lane fell, Burnside's men finally outflanked the Confederate position and crossed the creek. The Confederates fell back toward Sharpsburg. At 3:00 P.M., the Union troops began to advance.

A missed chance

McClellan still had two reserve corps he could send forward. Such a move now would have won the Union a great victory. But McClellan was naturally cautious. He hesitated—and the chance disappeared. Burnside's left flank was attacked by Confederates arriving from Harpers Ferry. Burnside fell back toward the creek.

The fighting ended as night fell. There was no clear winner, but the North probably had the advantage. It had halted the Confederate invasion. President Abraham Lincoln treated the battle as a Union victory. He issued his Emancipation Proclamation three days later.

Battle details of Union and Confederate troop movements.

BATTLE DETAILS

1. The Union attack on the Confederate left flank at dawn led to fierce fighting in the West Woods around the Dunker Church.

2. The battle shifted to the center of the Confederate line. At the sunken road, Confederates held off Union attacks for four hours before retreating at about 1:00 P.M. The position was named "Bloody Lane."

3. Union commander Ambrose Burnside crossed the creek and attacked at 3:00 P.M. as the enemy fell back. The arrival of Confederate reinforcements forced the Union troops to retreat in turn. The battle ended in a draw.

JANUARY 15, NORTH CAROLINA
Wilmington, the last port in Confederate hands, is closed.

JANUARY 19, SOUTH CAROLINA
General Sherman vows to march through the Carolinas.

JANUARY 31, VIRGINIA
Robert E. Lee is named general-in-chief of all the Confederate armies.

JANUARY 4, UNITED STATES
The New York Stock Exchange opens its first permanent headquarters.

JANUARY 27, PERU
Peru's independence is established in a treaty with Spain.

JANUARY 31, UNITED STATES The House of Representatives approves an amendment to the Constitution abolishing slavery; it will become the Thirteenth Amendment.

Battle of Fredericksburg

In December 1862, a new commander of the Union Army of the Potomac decided to cross the Rappahannock River to make another advance on the Confederate capital at Richmond.

A lithograph of the Union Army shows it as it crosses the Rappahannock River to Fredericksburg.

The new Union commander was Ambrose E. Burnside. He had been appointed by President Abraham Lincoln on November 7, 1862, to replace General George B. McClellan. Lincoln had become frustrated with McClellan's cautious

1865
February–March

CIVIL WAR

FEBRUARY 3, VIRGINIA
President Lincoln and Confederate representatives fail to agree on a diplomatic ending to the war.

FEBRUARY 16, SOUTH CAROLINA
Columbia surrenders to General Sherman's Union troops.

FEBRUARY 17, SOUTH CAROLINA
As Union troops enter Columbia, someone sets fire to cotton bales across the town. Over half of the city is destroyed.

FEBRUARY 27, KENTUCKY
Confederate guerrilla leader William C. Quantrill and his band attack civilians in Hickman.

OTHER EVENTS

FEBRUARY 12, UNITED STATES
Henry Highland Garnet becomes the first African American to speak in the House of Representatives.

FEBRUARY 22, UNITED STATES
Tennessee adopts a new state constitution that outlaws slavery.

February

approach. He wanted Burnside to be more aggressive. Burnside planned a winter advance toward Richmond, crossing the Rappahannock River at Fredericksburg.

Crossing the river

When Burnside reached the opposite bank of the river from Fredericksburg on November 19, he found that the bridge over the Rappahannock had been destroyed. His huge army—some 120,000 men—had to halt. On the other side of the river, the delay gave Robert E. Lee time to position an army of 90,000 men on Marye's Heights, high ground from which they could cover every inch of ground to the river.

On December 11, Burnside finally crossed the river; he occupied the city over the next two days. The next task was to assault the Confederate line. By 9:00 A.M. on December 13, two divisions had advanced, only to be pinned down by Confederate fire at the foot of the ridge. They were later driven back by a counterattack.

Impregnable position

Union infantry tried 14 more times to charge the heights. Each time, they failed. Burnside wanted to order more attacks, but was persuaded not to. The next day he ordered his troops back across the river. He had lost 12,000 men killed or wounded, against Confederate losses of 4,700. The South had won.

Union forces occupied the town (1) but assaults on Prospect Hill (2) and Marye's Heights (3) failed.

MARCH 2, VIRGINIA
The Shenandoah Valley is in Union control after the Confederates lose the Battle of Waynesboro.

MARCH 3, WASHINGTON, D.C. The U.S. Congress sets up the Freedmen's Bureau to help deal with the problems resulting from the sudden freeing of tens of thousands of slaves.

MARCH 13, RICHMOND
The Confederate Congress passes a law authorizing the use of black troops.

MARCH 19, NORTH CAROLINA
Joseph E. Johnston attempts to stop the march of Union general William T. Sherman through the Carolinas in the Battle of Bentonville; he is defeated late the following day.

MARCH 4, UNITED STATES
Abraham Lincoln is inaugurated for his second term as president.

MARCH 18, SOUTH AMERICA
Paraguay goes to war with the Triple Alliance of Brazil, Argentina, and Uruguay.

Battle of Murfreesboro

In the West, New Year 1863 saw some of the most intense fighting of the war as the Union attempted to strengthen its position in central Tennessee and Kentucky.

Union and Confederate forces shown fighting at the Battle of Murfreesboro.

The Union Army of the Cumberland had gone on the advance in December 1862. Its commander, William S. Rosecrans, was seeking a decisive battle over the Confederate Army of Tennessee, under General Braxton Bragg. Rosecrans's army

1865 April–May

CIVIL WAR

APRIL 1, VIRGINIA
The Battle of Five Forks ends in defeat for the Confederate Army of Northern Virginia.

APRIL 2, VIRGINIA
Grant attacks Petersburg and the Confederates start a retreat from Petersburg and Richmond.

APRIL 6, VIRGINIA
Lee loses 8,000 men to Union attacks at the Battle of Sayler's Creek.

APRIL 7, VIRGINIA
Grant asks Lee for his army's surrender; Lee asks for terms.

APRIL 9, VIRGINIA
Lee surrenders to Ulysses S. Grant at Appomattox Courthouse.

OTHER EVENTS

APRIL 21, UNITED STATES
Lincoln's funeral train leaves Washington, D.C.; it will popularize the Pullman sleeping car.

April

moved south from Nashville to meet Bragg at Murfreesboro, Tennessee. By December 30 the two armies faced each other near Stone's River.

The two sides' battle plans mirrored one another: an attack on the enemy's right flank. The Confederate assault was more successful. From dawn the next day, it putshed its opponents back over 2 miles (3.2 km). At nightfall Bragg sent a telegram to Richmond to report that the Union was in full retreat.

The Union right flank under attack at the Battle of Murfreesboro, December 31, 1862.

But Rosecrans had fallen back in good order. Dawn revealed the Union army still in position— much to Bragg's surprise. After a day's rest on New Year's Day, Bragg ordered an assault on an isolated part of the Union line on January 2. Not only was the attack turned back; Bragg also thought that Rosecrans had received reinforcements. He was mistaken—but on the morning of January 3, Bragg ordered the Army of Tennessee to retreat.

Hard-fought victory

The Battle of Mufreesboro was among the hardest fought of the Civil War. Of Bragg's 35,000 troops, more than a quarter were killed or wounded. The Union losses were a little lower— 23 percent of 41,400 men. But the battle had been a strategic victory for Rosecrans. It left Union forces in control of Kentucky and secured their hold on Tennessee.

APRIL 14, WASHINGTON, D.C.
President Lincoln is shot while watching a play at the theater.

APRIL 15, WASHINGTON, D.C.
Lincoln dies from his injuries; Vice-President Andrew Johnson becomes president.

APRIL 26, NORTH CAROLINA
Confederate General Joseph E. Johnston surrenders to General William T. Sherman.

MAY 10, GEORGIA
Confederate President Jefferson Davis is captured and taken into custody.

MAY 29, WASHINGTON, D.C.
President Andrew Johnson grants an amnesty and pardon to Confederate soldiers who will take an oath of allegiance to the Constitution.

APRIL 27, TENNESSEE 2,000 Union soldiers aboard the riverboat Sultana die when it catches fire and sinks on the Mississippi River.

MAY 1, UNITED STATES
Walt Whitman publishes "Drum Taps," his long poem about the Civil War.

NEED TO KNOW

Some of the subjects covered in this book feature in many state curricula. These are topics you should understand.

People:
Abraham Lincoln
Jefferson Davis
Robert E. Lee
George B. McClellan

Strategy:
Blockade of the South
War in the West
Peninsular Campaign
Invasion of the North

Tactics & Technology:
Railroads
Ironclads
Cavalry
Infantry

KNOW THIS

This section summarizes two major themes of this book: the unequal distribution of resources and the strategies of the North and the South.

RESOURCES

INDUSTRY
The North had far more heavy industry than the South, which gave it an advantage in terms of railroads, weapons, and ammunition. That advantage became more important the longer the war lasted.

BLOCKADE
The Union blockade prevented the South from importing weapons; it also prevented the export of cotton, the South's most important trade crop.

FOOD
The South soon began to run low on food. This partly reflected the effectiveness of the Union blockade, but it was mainly the result of the disruption to agriculture caused when farmers went off to fight in the war.

POPULATION
The North had about 22 million inhabitants; the South had only about 9 million, including some 3.5 million slaves, who were not allowed to fight.

STRATEGY

- The North had virtually no time to train its volunteer army before it was defeated at the First Battle of Bull Run in July 1861.
- The Northern blockade was intended to slowly choke the South; the North would win a war of attrition.
- The North's priority in the West was to win control of the Mississippi River and the port of New Orleans, a vital trade link.
- The first naval battle between iron warships took place at Hampton Roads in March 1862.
- The North invaded the South in March 1862. It planned to march across the Virginia Peninsula and capture the Confederate capital at Richmond.
- After the South had managed to halt the Union offensive on Richmond, Robert E. Lee's Army of Northern Virginia invaded the North to threaten Washington, D.C.
- The Southern invasion was defeated at the Battle of Antietam (Sharpsburg) in September 1862; the first day of the battle was the bloodiest day of the whole war. The Union lost about 11,650 men killed or wounded; the Confederates lost about 9,300.

TEST YOURSELF

These questions will help you discover what you have learned from this book. Check the pages listed in the answers below.

1. How did "Stonewall" Jackson get his nickname?

2. What river was defended by Fort Donelson?

3. How were the crew of the Confederate ironclad *Virginia* surprised on the second day of the Battle of Hampton Roads?

4. Where was the Rebel Yell first heard?

5. How did the Hornets' Nest at Shiloh get its name?

6. What was General Butler's Order 28 in New Orleans also called?

7. Why did General George B. McClellan halt his advance on Richmond in April 1862?

8. Who replaced Joseph E. Johnston as commander of the Confederate Army of Northern Virginia?

9. How did General McClellan gain an advantage at Sharpsburg?

10. What river guarded the Confederate position at Fredericksburg?

ANSWERS

1. For his solid defense at the Battle of Bull Run (see page 8). 2. Cumberland River (see page 11). 3. By the appearance of a Union ironclad, the *Monitor* (see page 13). 4. Fort Donelson (see page 16). 5. From the buzzing sound of bullets (see page 16). 6. The "Woman's Order" (see page 19). 7. He thought he faced a far larger enemy than he actually did (see page 21). 8. Robert E. Lee (see page 25). 9. He saw Lee's orders (see page 37). 10. Rappahannock (see page 41).

GLOSSARY

artillery Heavy guns such as cannons that fire shells and balls a long way.

batteries Groups of heavy guns, such as cannons.

bayonet A sharp dagger that is attached to the end of a rifle for hand-to-hand fighting.

blockade Measures aimed at preventing trade by using ships to intercept vessels heading toward port.

bombardment A period of artillery fire aimed at a particular target.

brigade A military unit made up of about 5,000 soldiers divided into two to six regiments.

cavalry Soldiers that fight on horseback.

counterattack An attack launched on the enemy after he has already attacked.

division The largest unit of an army: it is made up of three or four brigades.

entrench To dig in to a defensive position.

flank The side of a military unit or line.

fortifications Positions that are protected by strong defenses such as trenches or walls.

garrison A group of soldiers who occupy a military post.

infantry Soldiers who fight on foot.

ironclad A ship that is protected by a covering of iron armor.

militia Part of a country's army made up of citizens who are called on to serve in times of emergency.

regiment A military unit; at full strength, a regiment had 10 companies of 100 men.

rout A total defeat.

siege A military attack in which an army or city is surrounded and cut off in order to force its surrender.

skirmish A minor fight between enemy forces.

torpedo The name used during the Civil War for mines, hidden explosive devices used to destroy enemy transportation, such as ships.

FURTHER READING

BOOKS

Beller, Susan Provost. *Billy Yank and Johnny Reb: Soldiering in the Civil War* (Soldiers on the Battlefront). Twenty-First Century Books, 2008.

Hama, Larry. *Surprise Attack! The Battle of Shiloh* (Graphic History). Osprey Publishing, 2006.

Hama, Larry. *The Bloodiest Day: Battle of Antietam* (Graphic History). Osprey Publishing, 2006.

Hama, Larry. *The War is On! Battle of First Bull Run* (Graphic History). Osprey Publishing, 2007.

Kostyal, Karen. *1862, Fredericksburg: A New Look at a Bitter Civil War Battle*. National Geographic, 2011.

Morris, Gilbert L. *Encounter at Cold Harbor* (Bonnets and Bugles Series no. 8). Moody Press, 1997.

Riddleburger, Sam, and Michael Hemphill. *Stonewall Hinkleman and the Battle of Bull Run*. Dial, 2009.

Shah, Ruchir. *The Civil War*. EZ Comics, 2007.

Sheinkin, Steve. *Two Miserable Presidents: Everything Your Schoolbooks Didn't Tell You About the Civil War*. Roaring Brook Press, 2008.

Stanchak, John E. *Eyewitness Civil War*. Dorling Kindersley, 2000.

WEBSITES

www.civilwar.com
Comprehensive privately run, moderated site on the Civil War

www.civil-war.net
Collection of images, written sources, and other material about the Civil War

www.historyplace.com/civilwar
The History Place Civil War timeline

www.pbs.org/civilwar
PBS site supporting the Ken Burns film *The Civil War*

www.civilwar.si.edu
The Smithsonian Institution's Civil War collections, with essays, images, and other primary sources

INDEX